D0478728

# STREAMING TV

CHERRY LAKE Publishing

Published in the United States of America by Cherry Lake Publishing
Ann Arbor, Michigan
www.cherrylakepublishing.com

Content Adviser: Jessica Haag, MA, Communication and Media Studies
Reading Adviser: Cecilia Minden, PhD, Literacy expert and children's author

Photo Credits: ©Rawpixel.com/Shutterstock.com, Cover, 1; ©NASA/Photo no. E49-54, 5; ©Yevhenii Orlov/
Shutterstock.com, 6; drserg/Shutterstock.com, 7; ©Tiffany Bryant/Shutterstock.com, 9; ©Mat Hayward/
Shutterstock.com, 10; ©Avdmg/Wikimedia Commons, 13; ©Rawpixel.com/Shutterstock.com, 15; ©Davizro
Photography/Shutterstock.com, 16; ©DiegoMariottini/Shutterstock.com, 19; ©lithian/Shutterstock.com, 20;
©Casimiro PT/Shutterstock.com, 21; ©Happy Together/Shutterstock.com, 22; ©pixinoo/Shutterstock.com, 25;
©Happy Auer/Shutterstock.com, 26; ©DFree/Shutterstock.com, 27; ©YAKOBCHUK VIACHESLAV/
Shutterstock.com, 28

Library of Congress Cataloging-in-Publication Data

Names: Mara, Wil, author.
Title: Streaming TV / by Wil Mara.
Description: Ann Arbor : Cherry Lake Publishing, [2018] | Series: Global citizens. Modern media |
    Includes bibliographical references and index. | Audience: Grades 4 to 6.
Identifiers: LCCN 2018006958 | ISBN 9781534129320 (hardcover) | ISBN 9781534132528 (pbk.) |
    ISBN 9781534131026 (pdf) | ISBN 9781534134225 (hosted ebook)
Subjects:  LCSH: Streaming technology (Telecommunications)—Juvenile literature.
Classification: LCC TK5105.386 .M37 2018 | DDC 384.550285/4678—dc23
LC record available at https://lccn.loc.gov/2018006958

Cherry Lake Publishing would like to acknowledge the work of the Partnership for 21st Century Learning.
Please visit *www.p21.org* for more information.

Printed in the United States of America
Corporate Graphics

## ABOUT THE AUTHOR

Wil Mara has been an author for over 30 years and has written more than 100 educational titles
for children. His books have been translated into more than a dozen languages and won numerous
awards. He also sits on the executive committee for the New Jersey affiliate of the United States
Library of Congress. You can find out more about Wil and his work at www.wilmara.com.

# TABLE OF CONTENTS

# CHAPTER 1

# History: How Streaming Came into Existence

People have been communicating with each other for thousands of years. What began as rock carvings has slowly changed into books, newspapers, magazines, movies, radio, TV, and the Internet. Together, they are called **media**.

One of the most popular ways people get their media is by **streaming** it from the Internet. People stream television, movies, music, and even books! They can do this almost anywhere in the world, thanks to streaming technology. But it wasn't always so easy to access media this way.

The term "computer" used to refer to a person who solved math by hand.

## Early Days

Attempts to stream media date back to the late 1800s. The first to attempt "streaming" were Guglielmo Marconi and Nikola Tesla, inventors of long-distance radio. By 1927, Philo Taylor Farnsworth invented a way to wirelessly transmit digital images from one place to another. This was the beginnings of television. With the invention of the first **programmable** computer during the 1930s and the Internet in the late 1960s, streaming media became more of a reality. In 1995, Progressive Networks, an Internet-based

There are still 9.4 million people in the United States that use dial-up.

Tim Berners-Lee invented the first Internet browser in 1990.
It was called WorldWideWeb.

media service provider, became the first to stream audio online
for the public. The audio was of a baseball game between the
New York Yankees and Seattle Mariners. Five years later, the
company (renamed RealNetworks) provided more than 85 percent
of the streaming content online.

In 1997, other companies were developing better and faster
ways to stream audio and video. To do this, they needed to increase
the Internet **bandwidth**. At this time, most people were using
**dial-up** to connect to the Internet. Dial-up connections didn't

require anything other than a telephone line. It was cheap and accessible, but it was incredibly slow. Most videos were unable to properly stream.

## Into the New Millennium

Microsoft took over the streaming technology field during the early 2000s when it dominated the computer industry. RealNetworks's media player was free to download and use, but customers had to pay to unlock certain features. Microsoft gave away these features for free. The media player came preinstalled on Microsoft's Windows **operating system**, which was on almost all personal computers.

The demand for streaming media increased, but actually streaming media was becoming more difficult. This all changed in 2007. Around this time, **broadband** started to replace dial-up. A company discovered a way to stream media online without having to rely on Internet bandwidth. This revolutionary discovery, paired with high-speed Internet access, helped speed up video **buffering** times and connection issues.

TV shows were starting to pop up on the Internet around the mid-2000s.

About 61 percent of U.S. young adults ages 18 to 29 primarily use online streaming platforms to watch television.

## Streaming Today

Today, concerts can be viewed live and people in different parts of the world can chat face-to-face by video conferencing. Music, movie, and television streaming services are being used more than ever. Television is one of the most popular media that people stream. Between 2005 and 2008, advances in streaming technology led to big changes in television. Networks that **broadcast** television started losing money because its viewers were choosing to stream content online rather than watch it on TV.

By 2014, about 30 million U.S. homes had Internet **set-top** devices, such as Roku, Chromecast, and Apple TV. That same year, 45 percent of people who paid for TV reduced their services and 8 percent canceled their services. Three years later, 22.2 million Americans had completely canceled TV services. In 2017, it was estimated that 34.4 million American adults never had television services, like broadcast or cable, to begin with. This disruption comes from **over-the-top** (OTT) streaming businesses, like Netflix, Hulu, and Amazon Prime Video. In fact, Netflix was to blame for half of the decline in TV viewership in 2015!

## Developing Questions

*Two reasons streaming television became so popular so quickly are convenience and the ability to customize it to one's lifestyle. People can watch shows they like, on a device of their choosing, and at a time that's convenient for them. What other personalized aspects of streaming do you think will be developed in the future?*

# CHAPTER 2

# Geography: Streaming Around the World

In an age of instant information, the demand for streaming media has grown at an incredible pace. Many people are used to accessing virtually anything online. But not all parts of the world access the same content.

## China

China has long controlled and filtered Internet content. Its government has enacted more than 60 Internet-related regulations. For instance, people in China have been banned from accessing YouTube since 2009. In June 2017 alone, China banned the online

An Internet-based "rap reality" TV show in China pulled in more than 2.5 billion views!

video services on some of its media sites and 12 live-streaming apps. As of September 2017, the country requires drama series that are streamed online to obtain a government permit. Without one, its fans will be unable to stream the series.

Despite these strict regulations, video streaming continues to gain popularity there. It might be because China focuses on Chinese-based content. Its broadcasters and streaming services can only dedicate 30 percent or less of their content to foreign movies and shows. While the country doesn't have access to

YouTube, it does have Youku. Youku streams everything from music videos and movies to full episodes of cartoons and TV shows. iQIYI is another online video service. More than 100 million Chinese users access Youku and iQIYI through mobile devices.

## Africa

People in developing nations can also stream television online. While many areas of Africa don't have cable television, they are getting more Internet access. This allows citizens to stream TV shows they've been missing. In 2016, 16 percent of the continent had Internet access. This means about 160 million African citizens have the ability to go online. YouTube is one of the most-visited websites in Africa. In 2011, NollywoodLove, a Nigerian YouTube channel, was the first major channel to stream the most recent African movies. This channel has the most subscriptions of any channel in Nigeria. It attracts more than 1.2 million views from countries all over the world every month!

The 49 percent of South Africans who do not subscribe to a streaming service say they don't because they view the content illegally, can't afford it, or their Internet connection is too slow at home.

In 2017, Mexico had the most citizens watching Netflix every day.

## Netflix and India

India is another country with limited access to high-speed Internet. Because of this and the limitations in bandwidth, people have been unable to stream video. However, Netflix is looking to change this. It is planning to partner with **Internet service providers** in order to introduce people in India to better video streaming capabilities. If this project is successful, Netflix will introduce this technology to the Middle East, Latin America, and parts of Asia.

## Gathering Evidence and Evaluating Sources

*Developing countries aren't the only areas that have limited access to broadband Internet. In the United States, 28 percent of people living in **rural** areas don't have access or are unable to afford high-speed Internet. Even in **urban** areas, about 23 percent of Americans don't have high-speed Internet. In New York City, 1.6 million people don't have broadband Internet. That means almost 19 percent of the city's total population are unable to stream media. Why do you think this is? Do you think it's important for everyone to have access to high-speed Internet? Why or why not? Using the Internet and resources at your library, find out what the government, cities, and businesses are doing to help connect these people to broadband Internet.*

# CHAPTER 3

# Civics: Behind the Screen

Just about everyone enjoys watching a TV show or movie. With all the different content available, sometimes it's hard to choose what to watch. Because of this, many streaming companies are working on advancing the technology to better customize our TV- and movie-watching experience. But some people choose to watch **pirated** shows and movies instead of paying for a streaming subscription.

## Netflix Knows You

OTT streaming platforms collect data about their users. This data—like what you watch and how often—is analyzed and compared to the information it gathers from other users. Companies like Netflix do this in order to better customize

With in-flight wireless Internet on the rise and people choosing to stream video on their own device, more airlines are phasing out airline TV entertainment.

their recommendations. The data also helps them decide what types of content to make available and what types of original content to produce.

Netflix used its data to post a lighthearted comment on Twitter in 2017. The tweet was directed to 53 people who had watched *A Christmas Prince* 18 days in a row. Though intended as a joke, it backfired. Netflix had basically confirmed it was watching people watch movies. Users were upset. Before 2013, companies were unable to access this type of data and share it. That's because of the Video Privacy Protection Act (VPPA) that was passed in 1988.

About 70 percent of Netflix users watch multiple episodes in a row.

Montana residents streamed more hours of Hulu content than any other state in the United States in 2017.

The VPPA was intended to protect the privacy of consumers. In 2013, it was amended, thanks to Netflix and its users. The company had persuaded its users to pressure lawmakers to change the law so that people could share what they watch on Facebook.

## Some Don't Pay to Press Play

Most people stream TV using paid-for services like Netflix, Hulu, and Amazon Prime Video. But not everyone wants to pay. According to a survey, about 14 percent of people admitted to streaming content that wasn't **licensed**. In other words, they

A survey shows that people are watching significantly more TV thanks to streaming services and the cultural phenomenon of binge-watching.

watched something for free when they should have paid for it. Although 86 percent of users haven't streamed pirated content, 23 percent admitted they haven't because they didn't know how to. And 32 percent said they haven't because they think doing so is illegal.

In most cases, streaming unlicensed content is legal—at least for now. The websites that **host** the unlicensed content, however, aren't. According to a study, there were about 77.7 billion visits to these illegal streaming websites in 2016. Most people visiting these sites are from the United States, Brazil, and the United Kingdom.

## Developing Claims and Using Evidence

*With streaming television, it's easier than ever to* **binge-watch**. *A 2016 study revealed that 90 percent of* **millennials** *and 88 percent of those in* **Generation Z** *binge-watched a TV show at some point. According to another study, younger generations in Canada tend to binge-watch more than older generations. Using the Internet and resources at your library, research why young people tend to engage more in binge-watching than older people. Use the evidence you find to support your answer.*

# CHAPTER 4

# Economics: What the Numbers Tell Us

Streaming movies and TV shows is a fast-growing industry. People can stream content on their smart TVs, smartphones, tablets, and computers from almost anywhere in the world any time of day. The rise of streaming television online means more opportunities for businesses to make and spend money.

## YouTube Helps TV

More and more people are quitting regular television and moving to streaming subscriptions. But this doesn't mean the television set is going away. Although most people stream YouTube content on their smartphones, others are watching it on their

People in the United States in 2017 spent about $9.55 billion on subscription streaming.

TV screens. According to a study, streaming YouTube clips on TV grew 90 percent in 2016 compared to the previous year. This is good news for broadcast television networks, like NBC, that were struggling against OTT competitors, like Netflix. The study found that people spent 30 percent more time watching NBC YouTube clips on a TV screen compared to a smartphone or laptop. This means that more **advertisers** will be looking to buy ad spots in the digital space rather than in traditional TV commercials.

According to a study, U.S. video ad spending in 2017 reached more than $13 billion. Mark Marshall, head of NBC's entertainment

Amazon Prime Video spent $1 billion to make *Lord of the Rings* into a TV show.

advertising sales group, claimed NBC had 50 percent more advertisers buying YouTube ads in 2017 than the previous year. Google also released a study suggesting that YouTube ads were far more effective than TV commercials.

## Streaming TV Is Booming

In 2016, more than 49 million U.S. homes were connected to **Wi-Fi** that used some form of OTT streaming service. Netflix leads the streaming industry, reaching about 75 percent of those 49 million homes. Netflix plans to spend approximately $8 billion

*The Crown*—a Netflix original series—is one of the most expensive TV shows produced, costing $130 million for the first season alone!

Every minute, 72 hours of video are uploaded to YouTube.

in 2018—$2 billion more than what it spent in 2017. It is spending more money on creating original content. This might be because

## Taking Informed Action

*Some streaming services offer a better deal for their customers than others, depending on what they like. Services might offer movies and television shows or live-streaming and sports games. If your family is trying to determine which service to go with, take a survey of everyone's preferences. Use their information in your search to make your decision. Will you be streaming through Netflix or YouTube TV, or using a set-top device, like Roku, Apple TV, Chromecast, or Amazon Fire TV?*

many movies and TV shows that Netflix had offered to users are no longer available. For instance, FX, a cable TV channel, started pulling more of its TV shows off streaming platforms. Instead, FX added those shows to its own online subscription service.

While Netflix is the industry leader, it does face a few worthy competitors. Amazon Prime Video reached 33 percent of homes that use OTT streaming services and spent about $4.5 billion in 2017. Hulu reached 17 percent of those homes and spent about $2.5 billion. But YouTube might be Netflix's biggest competitor. It reached more than half of OTT homes in 2016 and spent significantly less than Netflix. This is mainly because YouTube relies primarily on its users uploading content.

## Communicating Conclusions

*Before reading this book, did you know much about how streaming TV disrupted television networks and changed our viewing habits? Now that you know more, why do you think it's important to learn about the streaming TV industry? What struck you as the most interesting? Share your thoughts with family and friends. Ask them what they think of streaming TV.*

# Think About It

It used to be that TV shows could only be viewed when they aired. Now we can watch shows anytime after their original airtime. In fact, 46 percent of millennials now wait to watch a show after it has already aired on TV. Movies used to be shown in theaters for a few months before being released to DVD or streaming services. But in 2015, Netflix released a movie that it produced both in theaters and on its streaming platform.

Streaming television and movies has disrupted not only broadcast and cable TV, but also Hollywood. Netflix won its first **Oscar** in 2017 and plans to release about 80 original movies in 2018. Amazon Prime Video had released 15 movies in theaters by 2017. It received seven Oscar nominations and won three.

How else do you think streaming services, like Netflix and Amazon Prime Video, will disrupt the movie industry? How do you think the movie industry will compete against these streaming giants? Research this topic further and use the data you find online to support your answers.

# For More Information

## Further Reading

Heitner, Devorah. *Screenwise: Helping Kids Thrive (and Survive) in Their Digital World.* Brookline, MA: Bibliomotion, Inc., 2016.

Green, Sara. *Netflix.* Minneapolis, MN: Bellwether Media, Inc., 2018

## Websites

**National Geographic Kids—Videos**
https://kids.nationalgeographic.com/videos
Watch a great variety of videos from funny to educational to awe-inspiring.

**Brainfeed**
http://brainfeed.org
Discover entertaining and educational videos.

# GLOSSARY

**advertisers** (AD vur tize-urz) people or companies that tell other people about a product or service in hopes of selling as many or as much as possible

**bandwidth** (BAND-width) the capacity for, or rate of, data transfer

**binge-watch** (BINJ-wahch) to watch many or all episodes of a TV series in rapid succession

**broadband** (BRAWD-band) of, relating to, or being a high-speed communications network; high-speed Internet

**broadcast** (BRAWD-kast) made public by means of radio or television

**buffering** (BUHF-ur-ing) accepting information (like data) at one rate and delivering it at another

**dial-up** (DYE-uhl-uhp) relating to or done using an ordinary telephone line

**Generation Z** (jen-uh-RAY-shuhn ZEE) the group of people born between the mid-1990s and early 2000s

**host** (HOHST) provide

**Internet service providers** (IN-tur-net SUR-vis pruh-VYE-durz) companies that provide their customers with access to the Internet and that may also provide other Internet-related services, like e-mail

**licensed** (LYE-suhnsd) having permission to have or do something

**millennials** (muh-LEN-ee-uhlz) the group of people born between the early 1980s and mid-1990s

**media** (ME-dee-uh) a method of communication between people, such as a newspaper

**operating system** (OP-uh-ray-ting SIS-tuhm) the software in a computer that supports all the programs that run on it

**Oscar** (OS-kur) award given by the American film industry to the year's best actors, movies, directors, and others; also known as an Academy Award

**over-the-top** (OH-ver-thuh-tahp) refers to streaming services that provide film and television content via high-speed Internet connections

**pirated** (PYE-rit-ed) content that has been reproduced without the owner's permission

**programmable** (proh-GRAM-uh-buhl) capable of being programmed

**rural** (ROOR-uhl) of, relating to, or characteristic of the country or country life

**set-top** (SET-tahp) referring to a device designed to link television sets to the Internet

**streaming** (STREEM-ing) watching or listening to video or music at the same time that it is being downloaded to your computer

**urban** (UR-buhn) of, relating to, or designating a city or town

**Wi-Fi** (WYE-FYE) the wireless signal that allows computers, smartphones, or other devices to connect to the Internet or communicate with one another

# INDEX